Refuge

Refuge

LA SEAN RICE

ISBN: 978-1-961017-68-9 (sc)
ISBN: 978-1-961017-69-6 (e)

Rev. date: 07/09/2023

CONTENTS

The day we got married was a magnificent date
As we fought through life's battlefield, we knew it was fate
Until death do us part, for better or worse, is what we had to state
When we got married, it was never a mistake
Our experience of things that took our love to the stake
The day we got married, it brought us new joy
God blessed our union, with another connection of our little boys
So I'm standing here years later, experiencing a rebirth
You are the gift to me on this earth
The day we got married, there was no snow in sight
As we caressed each other at the end of the night
In any marriage, couples tend to fuss and fight
Some push forward until they get it right
When we stood in front of God
With His love and His might
And professed our love to the world that we'll keep this tight
With pasted hurt, there were things that brought spite
We moved through those things without realizing the plight
I married you to complete my life
Never wanting anything more but you as my wife
I respect God, and know that I respect you
Fearing His power, yet realizing your view
When my eyes are closed, I often pray the bad times away
These God given powers of free will and to pray
And life together is where we will stay
Rebuking all the things that can cause us dismay
When we got married, it was our souls to take
Like God allowed Jesus to be nailed to the stake
I'm staying with God and His everlasting love for the rest of my days
And I will praise Him first for all the gifts that He gave
Surrounded by my family and love, as this was my fate
I want you know that's why I savor the date.

The Emotional Ride

Sitting in my car one day, thinking of taking a ride
I felt something strange that made me to look to the sky
Then asked myself what was happening, this feeling I felt I often denied
Missing those that are gone whom I used to confide
So I started up my car to take a drive
I continued to keep driving, taking my feelings in stride
Not giving them real thought so my mind could reside
These feelings got stronger and stronger, then became bona fide
They took over in an instant then I became blind
Controlling my spirit, body, and mind
I couldn't resist it, yet it was by design
My tone, my attitude, my heart, and my spirit couldn't find
So I drove on some more, resisting to feel this change
Fighting and resisting this feeling inside me that was so strange
Was I going crazy-a little, or feeling slightly deranged
What I felt, didn't come with any pain
Still fighting these feelings and voice that were talking to my brain
While driving, the sky became cloudy and it started to rain
Yet my spirit became lighter, releasing any thoughts of disdain
As I got stronger and stronger, I had to stop at a look
Using my mirror to see what it had took
Tears running from my eyes as my spirit had been shook
Thinking of the words that are written in the most infamous book
This emotional ride that I experienced right then
I had to pull over to let the process begin
Alone, no one could see the spin
Realizing that God's love had started to win
I gave up and rejoiced to allow my spirit to flow
Accepting and asking for forgiveness, letting all my pain go
Having love and joy embrace my spirit so
Driving with happiness on this emotional ride that I now know

100 Percent

I received a powerful word that redirected my world
Appreciating the fact it was given by blood
From someone whom I truly respect and love
Colonel Robinson, gave me something to glove
Accepting 100 percent responsibility and accountability for things I created
As a man thinketh is he, things became faded
Swallowing my pride, which had caused this disparage
Realizing this truth was just part of the damage
As a man, this was a hard pill to take
Hurting from memories that I knew weren't fake
100 percent responsible for my actions in all
Even hurting others who also hit a wall
Thinking, how could I take 100 percent?
Wearing many hats in my life, I have to consent
As the man of my home, like paying the rent
If things tend to fail, one should repent
Yet call it what it is to whatever extent
When you step back and realize that God's love is content
Doing things that are uncertain and trying to circumvent
Not accepting responsibility at 100 percent
Accepting this will make you stronger
You won't look to blame others any longer
As a man, other things can attribute to make you a king
Not just finding a woman and putting on a ring
Facing and dealing with all of what you have done
When I accepted this, my life had just begun
Creating a new man, a warrior who's ready and not spiritually gone
Competing and fighting until the battle is won
The man who accepts this can become a king
Accepting it all is sure to sting
When you do this as I have and truly not resent
Accepting the responsibility with 100 percent.

After the Storm

Thunder and lightning, roaring and crashing
Sounding off loudly, hearing nothing but smashing
Rain hitting the windows hard enough to hear
Usually after the storm, the sky becomes clear
The wind blowing ferociously, the wind chimes singing
With all the noise, your ears start ringing
Leaves on the trees, for their life they're clinging
As the rain hits the earth, a rainbow starts streaming
After the storm, there's often a calm
With raindrops you can collect inside your palm
Like the earth crying to heal from its pain
Continuing a rebirth and trying to remain
After the storm, my mission became clear
With you by my side, continuing to steer
Forward, toward love, not waiting at the pier
Opening up to you with love that's sincere
Through a natural disaster, my love will find you
Listen to your heart because it knows what to do
Embrace and grasp the feeling that's warm
My love for you will never die, even after the storm. . .

Alone

I remember one day I felt that I was alone
Having this feeling when we were on the phone
Realize, I felt like this because my heart had become stone
Not quite always respecting our love and watching my tone
My heart got harder and harder because of hurt from my past
Having you the rest of this life, is what has to last
Being alone is a real contrast
Wanting nothing but love and for you to grasp
When I'm alone, I often think of you too
If our love can get stronger than we ever knew
Asking for God's love to help bring us through
Understanding that our love was always true
"For better or for worse" is what we said
Having a few worse times, not love instead
With frustrating thoughts running through our head
When I began to get a grip, our love had slightly fled
Looking for your love with God's love to keep when alone in our bed
Not loving thy self, not getting my spirit fed
Receiving God's love, like what I had been read
Returning to His grace and love until we are dead
Alone, only because of decisions I made
Not opening my heart, from being hit with a spade
More is what I want for us—quality time, not shade
Rejoicing in love, grace, and happiness, enjoying life's parade.

As My Soul Mate

In the Bible, the soul is the spirit that is encapsulated in this vessel
When it finds a mate, it intertwines like a pretzel
With blood pumping through your veins, sometimes out of control
Then realizing for your soul mate, it's good for the soul
To feel a connection with someone you love, even when there's a disconnect
And to do all the right things to earn their trust, love, and respect
When you find your soul mate, you will feel the tension
Of any miscommunication, misunderstanding, and misdirection
That can take various forms and frustrate powerful unions
So a good connection is important to keep the communion
As my soul mate, it's time to this all right
Vowing to honor, love, and respect you every day and night.

Ask for a Dance

Chance after chance
I should have asked you to dance
Holding you close, moving, touching . . . feeling
Young hearts to old hearts, connected with love
And romance
My question, Can I ask you for a dance?
When my heart wants to ask
Yet my feet take a stance
Yet attempting to push my soul to ask for a chance
When I learned how to dance
Affection given, exposed this as part of romance
My arms in position to hold you firm and often close
By candlelight or moonlight whatever expresses the most
Just you and I, with no one yet God's in sight
Music made with our hearts, as it beats all night
Understanding this is part of romance
I think about how we used to dance
Though times in my life, I had to take a stance
Per stressing and unusual circumstance
Yet I would give to have another time, yet another chance
To ask you my love for a dance

Breakfast in Bed

Breakfast in bed is a sign of love and romance
Having breakfast with you is like an endless dance
Looking into your eyes with a stare, not a glance
Cooking with love and embrace; with a loving smile on your face
Thinking of the meal we're about to taste
To have breakfast in bed with you again and again
With our hearts eating, and feeding our souls so they mend
To express love this way and life to begin
Eating every bite slowly, not wanting to end
Walking to our bedroom to serve this to you
Having made something you enjoy yet every time appearing new
The great emotion inside the Most-High gave us two
To do just this for you is an overwhelming joy
A savory tasting breakfast can make lunch seem coy
As your face smiles when the skies are gray
Your stomach and your heart singing are part of the way
Having breakfast in bed with you to start a wonderful day.

Connection

You once said that you felt disconnected
Sly actions, words, and tones made you feel disrespected
When at times I felt often rejected
See, looking at the now and what is projected
That our steps from God were always directed
That the covenant we three made will always be protected
By forces more powerful than even expected
To do right, love God and our union—we accepted
We always have to work to stay connected
When we know that love and happiness should be reflected
Rebuking those things that sneak in undetected
The stuff that comes in and makes things get infected
Always loving thyself
Letting God correct it
Loving you is loving me, and is much respected
From the looks of things, I'm glad to inspect it
Let's step back to let God's love control, as directed
Which is the main ingredient to our love
When we're not connected.

Divine AND CONQUER

When I first attempted to conquer myself, I didn't know exactly what that meant
I did not realize that this entailed conquering things inside and out

When your inside is not good and your outside is good
There's a constant battle with yourself that can stagnate every part of your growth
One is unable to make certain moves
Really unable to get in the groove
With guidance, this would have been an easier task
Knowing what battles to fight, defeat, and leave in the past
What battles to take with a grain of salt
The battles that became wars—that was no one else's fault
Battles experienced not letting them go
That can become demons, which can stop your flow
Defeating them by not giving them any power to grow
When I realized these can ultimately destroy one's soul
Ridding those demons, reaching higher for God's glory to show
Fighting constantly inside, from what you've experienced
Letting go seemed as if it would be easy
Yet you find, several moons later, the demons were just hiding
Conquering yourself doesn't end quietly
Yet it makes you realize that happiness can be achieved
All the time and work, one must truly believe
That the Most High God will always have your back
Rebuking those demons from their vicious attack
This will happen if you let *HIM* truly divine and conquer yourself.

Dreams

When someone has a dream, it could go either way
It could be exciting, happy, or have lots of dismay
When you dream, there's often a message in store
With times and things that one can't ignore

Sometimes dreams can help your mind explore
Very frequently, they come, go, or often stay at the door
If the dream is happy, you keep your eyes closed, begging for more
Yet a nightmare is a dream that can prepare you for war

With this kind of dream, you think of evening a score
Yet frequently they come, go, and often stay at the door
You're just tired, maybe beat down, which can often make you snore
If you're snoring while sleeping really dream to adore

Being tired yet dreaming of something that's pure
Like watching the stars under moonlight by a fire, eating s'mores
Or a candlelight evening with love to deplore
Even cuddling by the fireplace, with our love at its core

A dream can have wonders in it that we don't want to miss
With happiness and joy you don't want to dismiss
The next time you dream, think love, don't let it resist
Often good dreams are signs of love that's sealed with a kiss

EMPTY NEST

One day, your home is full, and everyone's at rest
Then the next day, you come home to an empty nest
Wondering if you loved everyone right and gave them your best
If you walked and talked with nothing but love from your chest
Escaping the bad memories
For the ones that are fond
Thinking of happiness, like ducks in a pond
Hoping that through time, that love just respond
Waking up to an empty nest
Is not always good or bad thing
When you realize that your mission was really a quest
That the obstacles before you hurt and sting
Yet if you keep the course and do the Most-High's work
You can make changes and won't end up a jerk
Relax and do not act a fool or even go berserk
By changing your life, it can really work
Keep faith in front of you and be ready for a test
And keep love all around, especially inside your vest
When you think that you've lost and been beaten by the rest
Just find God, love, and joy, and fill your empty nest.

Energy Never Dies

It's said that energy is the one thing that never dies
Like the spirit of God that's not in disguise
That energy that lives on that most recognize
When things get tough, some often realize
The energy so strong that it can impale
To show nonbelievers that energy won't fail
It can lift you up when you feel kind of stale
Hold on to it tight as if it were a rail
I attest to this energy, for I know it's real
The God I know has made us a deal
If we honor and obey and vow to not steal
His power, love, and comfort are what we can feel
If we are part of God, that means we are energy too
We should look for His love when life gives us no clue
This energy, I hope and pray that you feel it too
Know that God's love is for all who believe it; that includes me and you.

Find and Seek

I've never seen anything as beautiful as I traveled the earth
Wondering if I would ever find it
Attempting to discover myself, I encountered various spirits
That acted as if they deserved mine
Yet time after time after time, I still couldn't find it
As I was seeking this beautiful spirit, I wished I could rewind
Years of being apart started to get to my mind
Eyes were blinded to the fact that if I attempted find it
Would I understand how the Most-High teach us to bind it
That beautiful coined spirit that I once knew and loved
As I find and seek it, there's only one love

Five Senses

The smell of your skin makes me want to have a taste
Like a fine wine you don't want to waste
Our touch of love is as thick as paste
Expressing my love to you, I will never haste

The void of your love, I would hate to face
When times I'm lost, is like I'm drifting in space
Vowing to complete my life with you until my resting place
Any ill thoughts of you are totally debased

Not being a man of the Most-High God would be an absolute disgrace
Looking at you, my love, and our family to not be displaced
So take my hand and my heart to feel my strong embrace
Hearing your voice in my ears, it runs straight to where my love is encased.

Forgiveness

When we ask for forgiveness
What does that mean?
To forget things that happened that aren't seldom seen
I asked the Most High God, and He wiped my slate clean
Getting back on track where my focus is real keen
As time goes on, you'll see what I mean
Forgiveness releases the hurt inside, from forming a cloud of steam
Clouding our hearts and minds like a bad dream
Make changes, be strong, and use your time to rebuild the team
Forgiveness from *Him* is the most power beam
When asking for forgiveness, things don't magically leave that day
I asked God if He would forgive me so I continued to pray
Forgiveness is given as a tool to reset, repair, and wipe tears away
I love you only and will show you each and every day.

Hands

When God gave us hands, He had a purpose
To pray, to build, to mold, and love those things given on the surface
To love those things that you can touch
To love those things that can touch back
To love those things that won't try to attack
To help lift the things that are heavy
To push and hold things, strong like a levy
To love the things you cherish
With love involved, anything will perish
Hands are used to serve and protect when needed
And never to disrespect anyone when heated
Hands are used to be gentle and kind
To love things with your body, soul, and mind.

Open-Heart Surgery

How do you mend a broken heart?
When it was practically damaged from the start
Being pushed and pulled like a shopping cart
It just wanted to be loved and enjoyed like art
When it received love, it made several mistakes
It was living and moving in a vicious state
Getting misused by others that just wanted to take
Few knew that your love was never fake
Then sirens went off, like during an earthquake
You wanted to stop it yet thought it was fate
Then realized it's your love they'd berate
Like food in the oven that continued to bake
With a high temperature, burning, feeling like you were cake
Looking forward to see what is really at stake
The sacrifice of love that's had its break
From love not known for you to equate
Reaching up high for some of God's love to rake
Hoping His love will help your heartache
If your heart starts hurting, just hit the brake
To find yourself in love with you before you hit the lake
To mend your heart and soul before it's too late.

HOW YOU SAY IT

We've heard this before
It seems that at times I didn't listen or understand completely
It's not what you say; it's how you say it
When words damage a beautiful soul, they can cut harder than a knife
Then your actions seem to lose control
Making memories not the best
When time is not moving out the added stress
There is no day or time when my words to you won't be kind
You are the love that cloud my mind
Real true love given by design
And yes, there's always going to be a test
I vowed to the Most High God that I will do my best
Pray, put armor around our family
Honor and obey *Him* relieving us from any stress
Leaving *Him* in control to do the rest.

I Awoke

One day I awoke alone in my bed
You being with me had gone to my head
Taking your love for granted, now my heart is not red
The way you made me feel, I'd trade that instead
You've done more than you know; my soul was being fed
Memories I thought I lost and want dead
Working hard to fix things and the words that I said
God woke me up to realize the truth
That without his love is an empty booth
Like having a headache from a sore tooth
Lovingkindness is what continues to rule
Being faithful and true has been my real tool
God's love can guide us to new routes
Getting back to our love and show the world what it's about
Building together, so our love can sprout
Promising to do better, praying to keep anger out
Our minds can be distracted, leaving some doubt
Giving you this poem is what I'm really about
I awoke alone with you not there
Picturing life with no love compare
I will submit, recommit, and strive to renew
Standing strong with God in our life first as we brew
I awoke this day to say I love you.

I Never Knew

I never knew that I could become erosive
With a traumatic past that has become explosive
With childish behavior that has become corrosive
I never knew that my reactions at times would be so emotional
The way that love was expressed to me was more physical
When I should have continued to be spiritual
Being better for you and our family
I'm striving to improve for you to see
That those things that held me back are moving out of me
For what matters is trust and honesty
Leaving things on the runway where they should be
Carrying honor, respect, and love with me
I never knew that I was capable of any form of hurt
Per my love had been broken and didn't want to work
I never knew
Rebuking enemies and demons that stole my token
With God as my support as the word is spoken
My heart aches for your love, which trauma has stolen
Understand that I didn't mean to hurt your heart
Using the power of prayer to do my part
Resetting, and preparing with a new start
Reaching high to the stars taking our love off the chart
Some ask for wisdom, knowledge, understanding which is really smart
Know you're the only woman with the key to my heart
I never knew that love was also a work of art.

I Repent

In the name of the Father, God
I repent
For my sins against our love that was sent
From God above, with His consent
To love, cherish, and honor thy wife with decent
For thy love was deceived by the serpent
That took our love through turbulence
Making it insecure with defense
Now I bring back the substance
To respect our God given covenant
With no type of control or constraint
My love is like the Most High; it's constant
Always striving to reconnect the distance
Anything but true love, I rebuke this instant
To open our hearts, minds, bodies, and souls for they deserve attention
For you, my wife, I will always strive for reconnection
Giving you honor, respect, love, and affection
Using time and energy into our love without deception
Being in love with you was my intention
So in the name of the Father, God
I repent
For my sins against our love, on which time was spent
From our God above, with His consent
To love, cherish, and honor thy wife with decent.

It Comes at a Cost

Most things in this life come at a cost
You don't get something for nothing, especially not from the Boss
When you think you have the answers and then appear to be lost
Know that searching is part of the toss
It comes at a cost when you don't realize the sacrifice
That we often overlook for not having any spice
Life is like craps; you keep rolling the dice
Looking back, not forward, then stopping to think twice
You keep spinning around, until getting stuck in a vice
Not walking upright similar to Christ
Hoping for nothing to happen when you think things are nice
Remember that Jesus was here, and it came at a price
It comes at a cost each and every day
When the wind is blowing and the rain causes dismay
I implore you, if things get tough, it's a good time to pray
And hope that God hears you and takes things away

Judge Me Not

Are you a judge? Are you a judge?
Judge me not; there is a Judge higher than the court system of the land
What you think of me is nothing
See, the way I see it, one can only be judged if one allows judgment to be cast upon them
Only if I allow the words and thoughts of others to act as an instrument to my existence
To navigate my thoughts toward or away from the judgment cast upon me
Judge me not if you have not walked a day or a mile in my shoes
Barring the pressures of this world that weigh the average person down or not paying my dues
Judge me not if your conscious mind is really unconscious, allowing negative energy to fill your vessel
Performing negative acts and movements in which your mind, body, and spirit have to wrestle
Judge me not if you do not believe in your higher self
That your understanding is limited to what you see and hear versus what you know
Judge me not if your inner temple is weak and crumbling, because your core never got strong
My core is strong and has fortitude; I gain my inner strength from God, my inner sun, my *chi*
As I expand into a supernova, enlightening, illuminating, and inspiring those who have not awakened their inner sun
Being a son of the Father, the Highest Power
I know that my greatness has already begun.

Kings and Queens

If a man is a king and a woman is a queen
Is there anything stronger that can go in between?
Two people of royalty—is it because they can afford bling?
Or because a queen wears a necklace and a king wears a ring?
Or because the honor they hold sometimes comes with a sting?
Making tough decisions that can often bring
About rough patches and frustrations or other kinds of things
Or being respected and gaining loyalty for what they've endured
Or because they stop just anyone from coming through their door
Or because they stand for each other, always ready for war
With true love in their hearts for others to adore
With a vision of their future together, ready to explore
Their souls bonded together; that they can't ignore
If you're a king, it's not a ring that gives you this honor, and it's not because you're a man
It's because a woman who's a queen gave you her hand
And a woman is not a queen because she found a man; she's a queen because the man and God have taken a stand.

Kiss

The first time that I kissed you
You said that I was the one who could kiss
Your soft lips touching mine is often missed
I love kissing you with love and passion
I wouldn't and don't care where, just in an intimate fashion
I hope that kissing you more will help show you how I feel
Never to confuse or break the deal
Of that covenant stated with our vows that remain
Our first kiss was heart felt nowhere near strange
Yet it was a feeling that I hadn't experienced
The more we got to know each other, the more that kiss became love
I think we both knew it was from up above

One Dimension

Hello, are you there?
It often seems as if I am the only one
Who looks at life as being serious yet often as an illusion?
When things that you can't control in this world you think is real affects everyone
Yet most of us wake up the next day to see the morning sun
What battle? What war?
As each day approaching has just begun
As an escaped slave wanting freedom is on the run
Music from *The Twilight Zone* is in your head, ringing softly, then loudly
As you lie there dead
Is it really one dimension, or more instead?

In this dimension, it's a lot of violence and chaos, not one day of peace
Not very often a moment for your spirit to increase
Looking at the time of the days past, yet in this dimension, they use an hourglass
Man, when you realize your time is limited, perspective kicks in
Of the many questions of what you did better or worse with your time
Which often moves fast when you have goals in mind
In this dimension, there are various species yet one human race
Yet the melanin of one's skin has become a disgrace
When the Most High has a serious price
Your love and your spirit to be the sacrifice
You shouldn't, yet in this dimension, you often think twice

From us who gave an oath for this country, to stand up and fight
Standing guard as warriors as our loved ones sleep through the night
In this dimension, there's been quite an imbalance
To sit and be regal, with wine in our chalice
Tonight I realize that every second is real

Is this the dimension in which I feel?
The emotions of love, then disdain, and what they reveal
Self-love with God's love is really the deal
As your time approaches, you must believe
That you have a real purpose that you have to achieve
In the world that we live in, you are given a choice
The conscious thoughts inside aren't just a voice
The spirit inside helps discern right from wrong
Bringing you to the true place where you really belong
I've met rebellion and resistance, those who have lost all faith
In which the time which we live is nowhere is safe
Facing the changing, challenging times and all of life's transitions
That's why it's hard for me to believe in this one dimension.

Suddenly

Waking up to an empty house
It was once filled
Now it's quiet and lonely
Not a sound of anything—love, laughter, children, or spouse
No one suddenly comes running to me
No greetings, no passion, no hugs, just myself to hang out with
Life flashes through my mind often as I sit by myself
Possibly feeling like my soul wants to be set free

Standing and looking in the mirror of life
There's often a reflection of trials that test you to the limit
Your insides feel hurt, yet you find the strength to keep moving
With a world that continues to move even when you're gone

Suddenly, various voices and images entered my mind
Consciously looking through a looking glass
Yet unconsciously being touched
Then a voice came again
It was words from the Divine
"Look at your life and the gifts I gave you
You're not alone; you have been found
You've finally realized the importance of the things I gave to you
The words that I speak will fester inside your soul
Release, let go, and let *Me* take control
I understand that having faith in *Me* is truly hard
Especially when in the midst of a storm and feeling off guard
Yet as you let go of things and stay close to *Me* through all your battles abroad
In the end, you will value *My* biggest reward
Eternal love and life that you have fought with a sword"
Walking and feeling *His* loving energy
To have true faith is a true testament of all time

Knowing that He has always been with me, even when I was my own enemy
Suddenly I stopped fighting; I let go and began to move toward
The energy, my faith blindly; that's spoken by His word

I turned around to look again yet let go of the past
Seeing a different sight in the looking glass
Touched by the spirit and voice of the Most High God
Thinking to myself and honoring the reward
Of feeling rejuvenated, energized, happy, and loved
Touching my soul, speaking to me in a monotone to be certain I could hear it
Suddenly, God raised me up with *His* grace and mercy, given by the Holy Spirit

Sunrise

I was driving along one day
And was able to see a beautiful sunrise
My eyes lit up with excitement
As I saw the sun rising from the horizon
As the sun illuminated the sky
Giving visibility to the trees, the grass, the plants, and the animals
Magnificent images were in my sight
As the sun was rising
My eyes wept slightly because I was unable to see
And experience this beautiful sunrise with you.

THE KEY TO MY HEART

You are the key to my heart
That I didn't know how to use
Not knowing how to use this key, I began to abuse
Yet this was the only one that I wanted to choose
The key loved me the most, per experiencing the blues
Not using the key right, I became kind of confused
At times to the point that I blew a fuse
The key wasn't as direct at times, dropping little clues
Poems written to you are a form of my muse
Other keys that I had didn't have the right tools
Now at this time in my life I don't have to choose
I often empowered my key and show it off
After trying to improve it
I shaped and molded from being dropped and scuffed
Yet it didn't want to change
Even just a little, so we could get through the door
Then I realized the key didn't want to try anymore
So the key referred a power to me
For the Most High can do anything
To believe in Him at all times
I wonder if I made it known from the start
That you are the true key to my heart